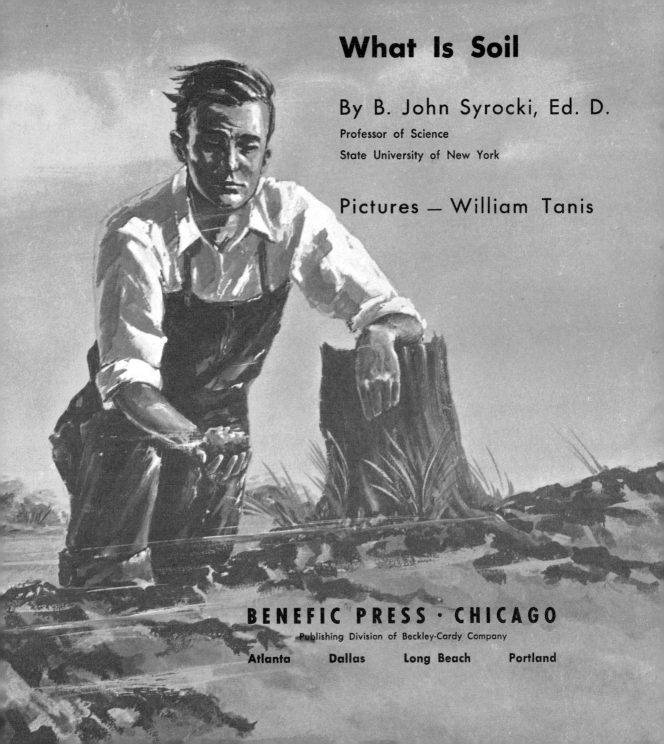

What Is Soil

By B. John Syrocki, Ed. D.
Professor of Science
State University of New York

Pictures — William Tanis

BENEFIC PRESS · CHICAGO
Publishing Division of Beckley-Cardy Company

Atlanta   **Dallas**   **Long Beach**   **Portland**

The WHAT IS IT Series

What Is A Bird

What Is A Cow

What Is A Fish

What Is A Frog

What Is A Plant

What Is A Tree

What Is Air

What Is Light

What Is Heat

What Is A Cell

What Is Water

What Is Sound

What Is A Star

What Is A Bee

What Is Soil

What Is Gravity

What Is A Rock

What Is A Season

What Is A Turtle

What Is A Chicken

What Is The Earth

What Is A Butterfly

What Is A Simple Machine

What Is A Magnet

What Is A Rocket

What Is A Solar System

What Is A Machine

What Is Chemistry

What Is Weather

What Is Electricity

What Is An Atom

What Is An Insect

What Is A Dinosaur

What Is Electronic Communication

Library of Congress
Number 61-6096

CONTENTS

THIS IS SOIL

Soil is the loose surface of the earth.
Soil forms a cover over almost all the earth.

Soil covers the hills.

Soil covers the bottoms of lakes,
of rivers, and of oceans.

Except for the tops of high
mountains and ice-covered regions,
soil forms a continuous cover
over the earth.

Soil in all parts of the world is not made of the same materials, although all soil contains rock particles.

Some soils are made almost entirely of rock particles. They are not good for growing plants. They are found in the desert.

Some soils contain decaying parts of plants.

They may also contain earthworms,

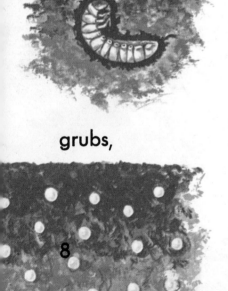

grubs,

air space,

and moisture.

bacteria and molds,

8

HOW SOIL FORMS

Rocks are slowly but continuously breaking down into smaller particles that form soil.

Rocks on the surface of the earth are broken into smaller particles. Soil forms where these small particles collect.

Rocks just below the surface of the earth may also break down into soil particles.

Rock materials are broken down into soil particles in different ways.

Continuous baking of rocks by the sun heats many rocks completely through. Heat causes the rocks to swell.

When rapid cooling follows during the night, the outside layers of rock cool faster than the inside.

Cold causes the rock to shrink. After weeks of heating and cooling, the uneven action causes the rock to peel and crack on the surface.

The rock is chipped.

Particles collect to form parts of new soil.

Rock materials are also worn away by the scratching of soil particles.

Sand usually contains quartz crystals which are so hard they can scratch most rocks.

Strong winds can carry sand particles very swiftly. The moving sand particles strike against rocks and chip them away.

Very slowly but continuously, winds and sand particles wear away larger rocks. The large rocks are broken down into tiny particles which fall or are carried off by the wind.

Water frequently fills the tiny cracks and crevices in rocks. Water freezing in the cracks of rocks will swell and push the rocks apart.

As the rocks break apart, more cracks are formed. These in turn are filled with water which may freeze, swell, and break the rock into even smaller parts. The rock slowly becomes part of the soil.

Plant roots may reach into the cracks of rocks and force them to break down even further.

Rain falls on rocks and the rain water combines with chemicals in the rocks.

Oxygen from water and from air combines with the iron in rocks to form rust. Rust makes the rocks softer.

Softer parts of rock are worn away by the beating rain and by the rubbing of particles that are carried by rain water.

13

Rocks under the earth's surface are being worn away slowly. When water trickles through the soil, it often combines with other chemicals and becomes acid. Water may combine with chemicals in the air during a thunderstorm and become acid. These weak acids can slowly wear away solid rock. A weak acid causes limestone to fizz and change into a softer substance.

In some places underground, limestone is worn away so much by acid that huge caves are formed in the rock.

When there is much vegetation and rain, soil contains. . .

decaying parts of plants,

animal wastes,

and decaying
bodies of animals.

This part of soil is called organic matter.

Parts of organic matter are broken down by the action of bacteria and molds. The decaying matter mixes with the topsoil.

Small bits of organic matter
added to topsoil help to separate
the tiny rock particles in the soil.
This lets air and water
enter the soil easily. Plants
need water and air to grow.

As the organic
matter decays, it
supplies plants with many of
the materials needed for growth.

HOW SOIL IS MOVED

Soil that remains where it was formed is called residual soil. However, soil on the surface of the earth may not have been formed from rocks in the region where it is found. Topsoil may have been brought from some other place.

Soil is carried from one place to another in different ways. Fast-moving streams carry very fine particles of sand and sharp pebbles.

Running water and sharp particles in running water cut into and loosen the soil along the banks of streams.

In this way soil is carried away to be deposited somewhere else.

Soil is deposited as the flow of running water slows down.

Large particles drop from the stream first. Lighter particles are carried the farthest.

Soil formed from particles released by a stream is called alluvial soil.

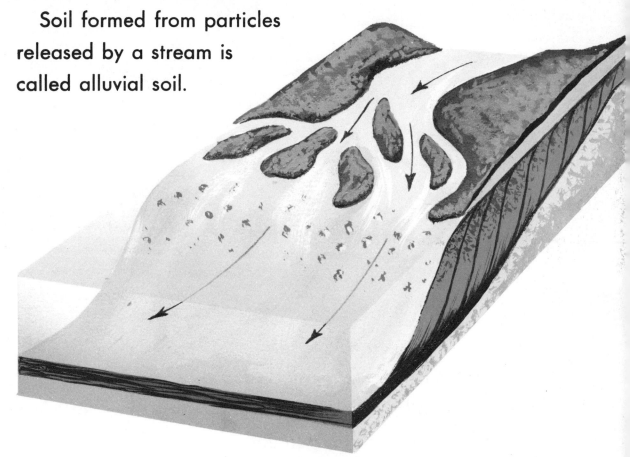

Soil left after flooding is made mostly of very fine particles called clay and silt. This is because fine particles are carried more easily by running water.

20

Much of the soil deposited around the Mississippi River is alluvial soil deposited during floods.

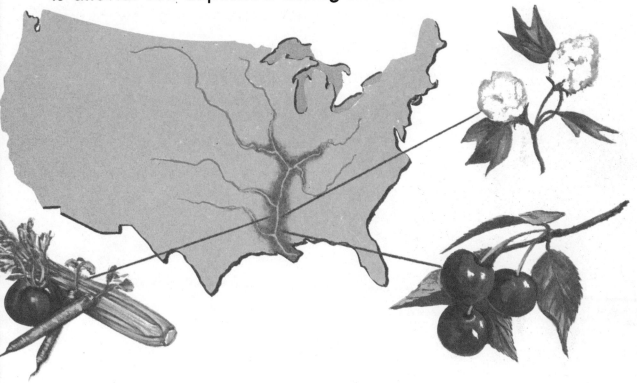

The region flooded by the river is known as the flood plain. The soil is generally rich in plant food and contains much organic matter.

Sometimes soil is moved only short distances. This often occurs on hillsides which have only a few plants growing on them.

During a rainstorm, raindrops loosen the entire surface which is washed slowly downhill.

22

Soil built up by oceans is marine soil.

Wave action slowly breaks rocks down into fine particles. The pounding of smaller rocks carried by waves aids in breaking down the larger rocks.

Rocks are broken down and eventually become sand particles.

After long periods of time, the land around the oceans may be gradually lifted by earth forces to form a coast.

The sandy soil once submerged in water is now above the ocean surface and makes up the new coastal region.

Soil is also moved by glaciers.

Glaciers are large masses of ice and snow that move down high mountains. As the glaciers move, the ice scratches away soil and rocks. The loosened rocks and soil are picked up by the moving glacier. The rocks picked up by the glacier help loosen and break other rocks as the glacier moves down the mountain.

25

When the glacier reaches the lower valley, it will usually melt away.

The soil which the melting glacier drops is called glacial soil. This soil is made of small pebbles, gravel, sand, and clay. It covers the topsoil that was there before the glacial soil was dropped.

Many years ago, glaciers covered much of the northeastern part of the United States.

As the glaciers melted away, soil and water were deposited.

The glaciers helped to form the Great Lakes and many smaller lakes in New England, New York, Wisconsin, Michigan, and Minnesota. Glacial soil was deposited in many places around the Great Lakes as the ice melted.

When there are only few plants on the land, the soil is not held together by plant roots. When there is little rain, the soil may become very dry and loose. This soil is easily blown away by strong winds.

Soil that has been carried by winds from one place and deposited in another is called aeolian soil.

After several severe dust storms, land may be covered by irregular drifts of soil. At times good topsoil as well as plants are completely covered. The land is useless.

SOIL IN DIFFERENT CLIMATES

Soil varies according to the climate in which it is found. If the climate is too hot and not enough rain falls, there will be few plants and animals. In the soil, there will be little organic matter in the form of wastes or decaying matter.

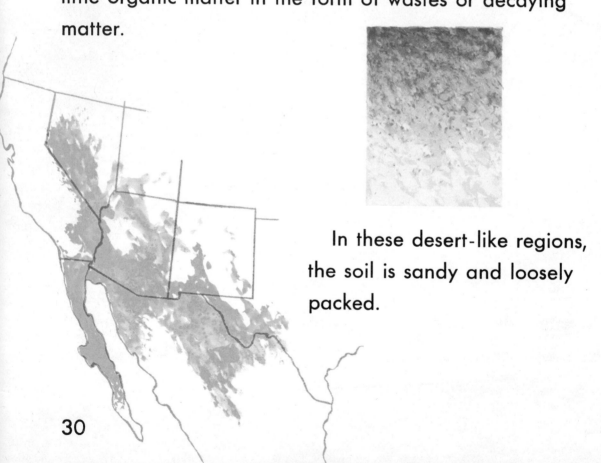

In these desert-like regions, the soil is sandy and loosely packed.

In the moist, warm areas of North America, the soil contains weathered rock and much organic matter. Many plants and animals add organic matter to the soil.

The organic matter may be in different layers of the soil.

Bacteria and fungi live on decaying matter, and continue to break down dead plant and animal remains.

Soon the fine particles of matter are carried by water deep into the topsoil.

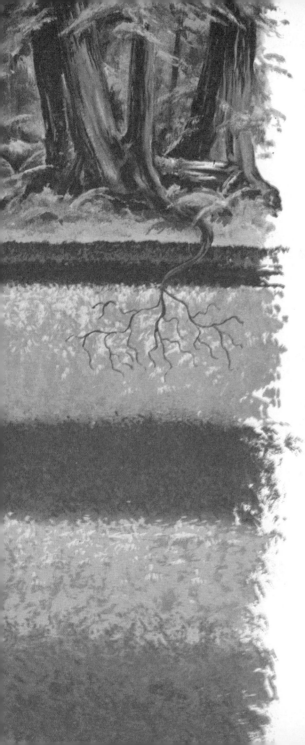

Rain and other climatic conditions may affect the soil in a different way.

Water seeping through the topsoil dissolves materials plants need for growth and carries these materials deep into the soil. Sometimes moisture carries plant food very deep. Some plants may not be able to reach these materials because the materials are carried too deep. When this occurs we say the soil has been leached.

This type of soil is very poor for farming.

This is the dark, rich land of the central part of North America. Our excellent wheat fields are located in this region. The yearly remains of plants add organic matter to the soil. Water does not carry the plant food too deep into the soil.

In the very cold or tundra regions, only the most hardy plants can grow. These are low shrubs and mosses. The layer of topsoil is thin since not too much weathering has occurred here.

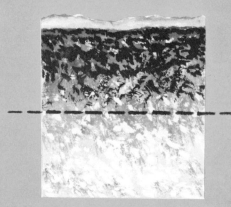

Below the layer of topsoil is a layer of permanent frost.

Soil in this region supports little growth. The ground stays hard and the amount of decaying matter in the soil is very small.

WAYS TO CONSERVE SOIL

It takes a long time for even one inch of soil to form. Each day rocks are being broken down into small particles by the action of wind, water, heating and cooling, and chemical action.

In some places, soil continues to form from rocks just below the surface of the earth. Oceans, lakes, glaciers, rain, and wind continue to move soil from one place to another.

It may take thousands of years to form one inch of topsoil. We must conserve the soil which is needed for the growing of food crops.

We need to make good use of soil.

High winds will not blow
this soil away. The roots of plants
hold soil particles down.

Water will not wash this soil away.

The roots of plants
hold the soil particles in place.

Here is a farm without vegetation.

The wind will pick up the loose topsoil and carry it away.

Water will wash away the good topsoil.
The wearing away of soil by wind and water
is called erosion.

Steep lands tend to
erode very rapidly.

Forests can prevent
rapid erosion. Roots of trees
hold the water and soil. The land
is protected. Trees are grown for
future use, and floods are lessened.

Different methods are used to prevent the wasting away of our soil. Strip cropping is one method. Farmers on the plains may want to allow part of their land to remain unplanted, but do not want to expose large areas of soil to the action of the wind. They plant strips of crop next to strips of open land.

The soil that is not planted is protected from the wind. This soil rests and soaks up moisture.

Strips of crops may also be planted across a slope. Plants which grow close together are planted in some strips. Plants which leave more ground open are planted in other strips. Rain water running down the slope is slowed down by the many plants in the heavily covered strips.

Contour plowing is used to reduce the amount of water that runs down a hilly area.

The land is plowed across the slope. Plants and furrows slow down the movement of water down the slope.

Water has a better chance to seep into the ground. There is less erosion of the land.

Fast-moving streams wear away banks. Soon part of a farmer's field is eroded away. Lining the banks of streams tends to reduce the wearing away of land. Soil is conserved.

Terraces are steps of level ground which are used to slow down water so that it may sink into the ground and not carry soil away as it runs downhill.

Each time the water reaches a terrace as rain or running water, it does not immediately start to run downhill. It has a chance to soak into the series of flat terraces.

As plants grow, they take water and other materials from the soil. They use the materials for growing and producing food.

Soils need fertilizer if they are to continue producing
strong, healthy, new plants. Fertilizers put back some of
the materials plants take from the soil as they grow.

The soil which covers the earth today began to form
long ago from rocky formations.

Soil for tomorrow is forming very slowly.

We must conserve this life-giving surface of the earth.

PICTURE DICTIONARY

DUST STORM   Strong winds carrying fine particles of soil. Page 29

EROSION   The wearing away of land surfaces by running water, wind, and glaciers. Page 38

GLACIER   A moving mass of snow and ice. Glaciers may move down a mountain and melt in a valley. Page 25

ORGANIC MATTER   Living material or material that at one time was part of a living thing. Page 15

TERRACES   Broad, flat areas across sloping land. Terraces slow down running water. Page 43

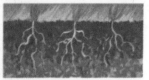

TOPSOIL   The top layer of soil in which most plant food is located. Page 15

VEGETATION   Plant growth. Page 15